NOV 1 9 2014

TOP HITS OF 2014

ISBN 978-1-4950-0091-1

HAL•LEONARD®
CORPORATION
7777 W. BLUEMOUND RD. P.O. BOX 13819 MILWAUKEE, WI 53213

Visit Hal Leonard Online at
www.halleonard.com

ALL OF ME

Words and Music by JOHN STEPHENS
and TOBY GAD

Moderately, with feeling

AM I WRONG

Words and Music by VINCENT DERY,
NICOLAY SEREBA, WILLIAM WIIK LARSEN
and ABDOULIE JALLOW

BEST DAY OF MY LIFE

Words and Music by ZACHARY BARNETT,
JAMES ADAM SHELLEY, MATTHEW SANCHEZ,
DAVID RUBLIN, SHEP GOODMAN
and AARON ACCETTA

Pop Rock

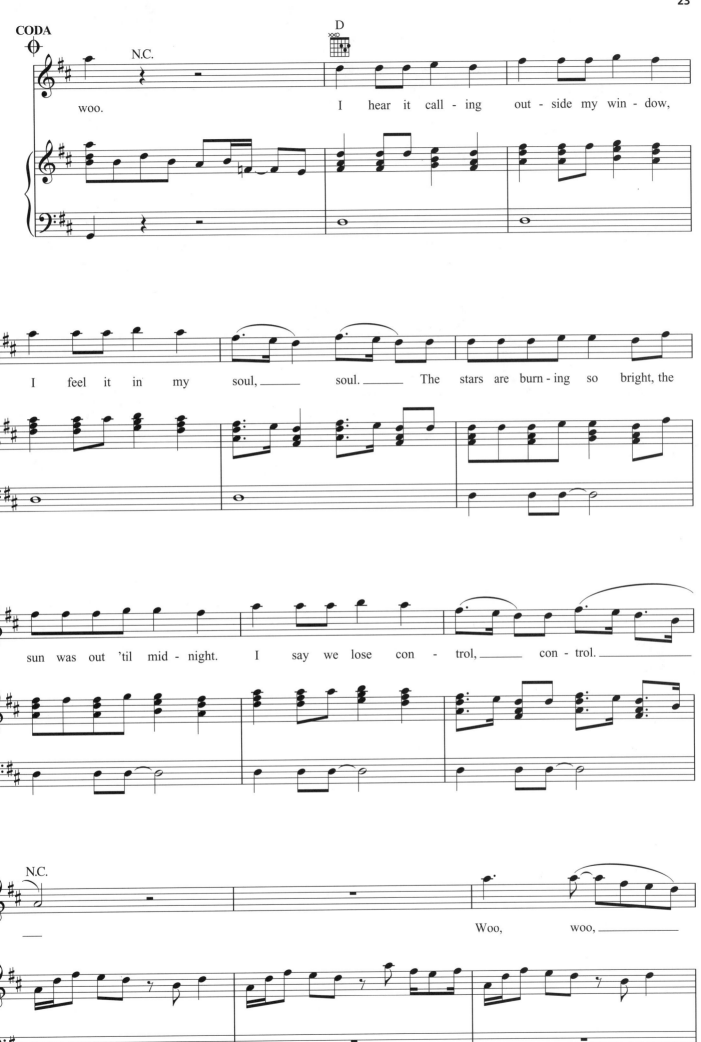

DARK HORSE

Words and Music by KATY PERRY,
JORDAN HOUSTON, LUKASZ GOTTWALD,
SARAH HUDSON, MAX MARTIN
and HENRY WALTER

* Recorded a half step lower.

FANCY

Words and Music by CHARLOTTE AITCHISON,
JONATHAN SHAVE, GEORGE ASTASIO,
JASON PEBWORTH, KURTIS McKENZIE,
JON TURNER and AMETHYST KELLY

Moderate Hip-Hop groove

Play 3 times

Rap 1: *(See additional lyrics)*

I'm so __ fan-cy, you al-read-y know. __ I'm in the __ fast __ lane

CODA

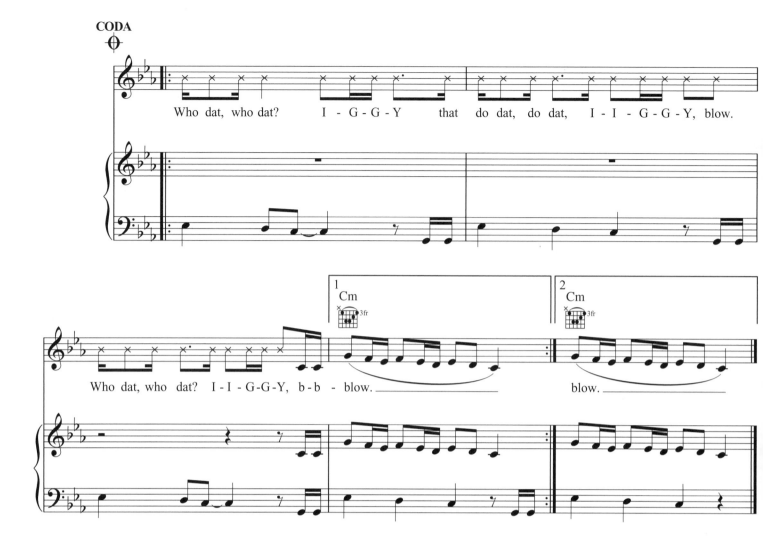

Additional Lyrics

Rap 1: First things first, I'm the realest, realest. Drop this and let the whole world feel it. Let 'em feel it.
And I'm still in the Murda Bi'ness. I can hold you down like I'm givin' lessons in physics. Right, right.
You should want a bad bitch like this, hah? Drop it low and pick it up just like this, yeah.
Cup o' Ace, cup o' Goose, cup o' Cris. High heels, somethin' worth a half a ticket on my wrist, on my wrist.
Takin' all the liquor straight, never chase that, never. Rooftop like we bringin' '88 back. What?
Bring the hooks in. Where the bass at? Champagne spillin', you should taste that.

Rap 2: I said, baby, I do this. I thought that you knew this. Can't stand no haters, and honest, the truth is
And my flow retarded. HPD departed. Swagger on suit but I can't shop in no department
And get my money on time. If they got money, decline. And swear I'm in that there so much, better give that line a rewind.
So get my money on time. If they got money, decline. I just can't worry 'bout no haters, gotta stay on my grind.
Now tell me, who dat, who dat, dat do dat, do dat? Put that paper over all, I thought you knew dat, knew dat.
I be the I-G-G-Y, put my name in bold. I been workin', I'm up in here with some change to throw.

Rap 3: Still stunting, how you love dat? Got the whole world askin' how I does that.
Hot girl, hands off. Don't touch that. Look at it, I bet you wishin' you could clutch that.
It's just the way you like it, huh? You're so good, he just wishin' he could bite it, huh?
Never turn down money. Slayin' these hoes, gold trigger on the gun like...

LET IT GO
from Disney's Animated Feature FROZEN

Music and Lyrics by KRISTEN ANDERSON-LOPEZ
and ROBERT LOPEZ

The snow glows white on the moun-tain to-night; __ not a foot-print _____ to be seen. _____ A king-dom of i - so-la-

Gaining confidence

HAPPY

from DESPICABLE ME 2

Words and Music by
PHARRELL WILLIAMS

Moderately fast

It might seem cra - zy what I'm 'bout to say:
Here come bad news, _____ talk - in' this and that.

Sun - shine, _ she's here; _
Well, gim - me all you got, _

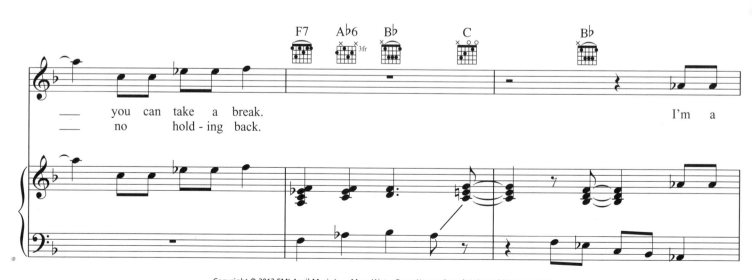

_____ you can take a break.
_____ no hold - ing back.

I'm a

LOVE NEVER FELT SO GOOD

Words and Music by MICHAEL JACKSON
and PAUL ANKA

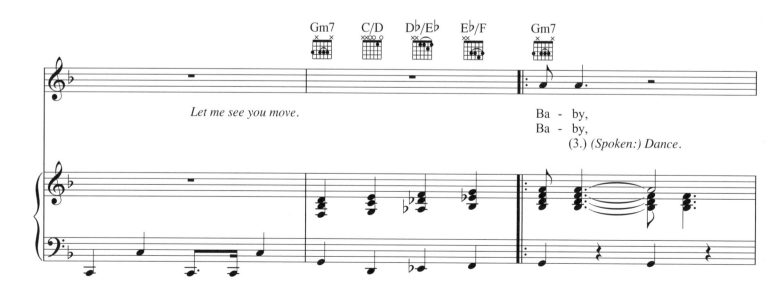

D.S. al Coda

RAGING FIRE

Words and Music by PHILLIP PHILLIPS,
GREGG WATTENBERG, DEREK FUHRMANN
and TODD CLARK

LOVE SOMEONE

Words and Music by JASON MRAZ,
BECKY GEBHARDT, CHASKA POTTER,
MAI BLOOMFIELD, MONA TAVAKOLI,
CHRIS KEUP and STEWART MYERS

72

POMPEII

Words and Music by
DAN SMITH

Moderately

Eh, ___ eh, oh, eh, oh. Eh, ___ eh, oh, eh, oh. Eh, ___

___ eh, oh, eh, oh. Eh, ___ eh, oh, eh, oh. Eh, ___ eh, oh, eh, oh. Eh, ___

___ eh, oh, eh, oh. Eh, ___ eh, oh, eh, oh. Eh, ___ eh, oh, eh, oh.

PROBLEM

Words and Music by ILYA, ARIANA GRANDE,
MAX MARTIN, SAVAN KOTECHA
and AMETHYST AMELIA KELLY

Recorded a half step higher.

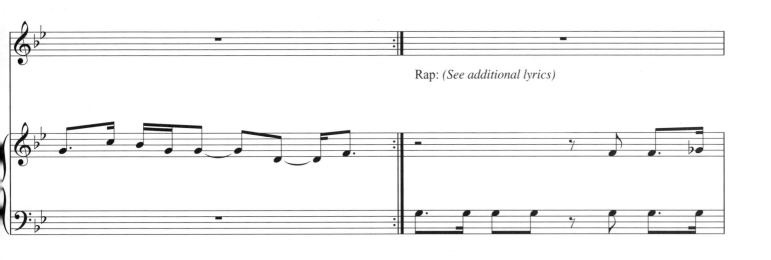

Rap: *(See additional lyrics)*

Additional Lyrics

Rap: Smart money bettin' I'll be better off without you.
In no time I'll be forgettin' all about you.
You sayin' that you know, but I really, really doubt.
You understand? My life is easy when I ain't around you.
Iggy, Iggy too biggie to be here stressin'.
I'm thinkin' I love the thought of you more than I love your presence.
And the best thing now is probably for you to exit.
I let you go, let you back. I finally learned my lesson.
No half-steppin', either you want it or you just playin.'
I'm listenin' to you knowin' I can't believe what you're sayin'.
There's a million you's, baby boo, so don't be dumb.
(I got 99 problems but you won't be one, like what?)

STAY WITH ME

Words and Music by SAM SMITH,
JAMES NAPIER and WILLIAM EDWARD PHILLIPS

SUMMER

Words and Music by
CALVIN HARRIS

Moderate Dance groove

When I met you in the sum - mer,

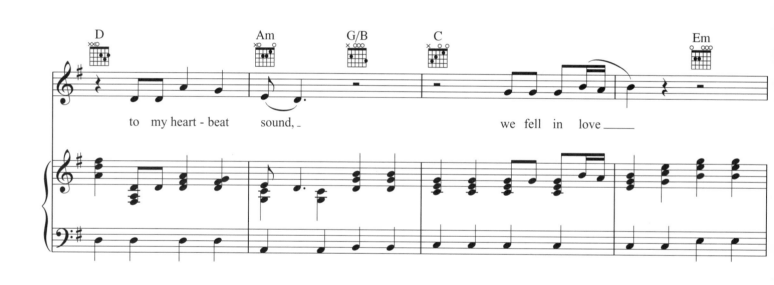

to my heart - beat sound, ___ we fell in love ___

as the leaves turned brown. And we could be to - geth - er, ba - by,

Sum - mer, ___

yeah.) ___

TIMBER

Words and Music by ARMANDO CHRISTIAN PEREZ,
PEBE SEBERT, KESHA SEBERT, LUKASZ GOTTWALD,
HENRY WALTER, BREYAN STANLEY ISAAC, PRISCILLA RENEA,
JAMIE SANDERSON, LEE OSKAR, KERI OSKAR and GREG ERRICO

Recorded a half step higher.

Additional Lyrics

Rap 1: The bigger they are, the harder they fall. This biggety boy's a diggety dog.
Have 'em like Miley Cyrus, clothes off twerkin' in their bras and thongs. Timber!
Face down, booty up. Timber! That's the way we like it. What? Timber!
I'm slicker than an oil spill. She say she won't, but I bet she will. Timber!

Rap 2: Look up in the sky, it's a bird, it's a plane. Nah, it's just me. Ain't a damn thing changed.
Live in hotels, swing on planes. Blessed to say money ain't a thing.
Club jumpin' like LeBron now. Voli, order me another round, homie.
We about to crown. Why? 'Cause it's about to go down.

SING

Words and Music by ED SHEERAN
and PHARRELL WILLIAMS

Recorded a half step higher.

deep, __ if an-y-bod-y finds out I'm meant __ to drive home. But I drink all of it, now I'm not.

So-ber-ing up, we just sit on the couch. __ One thing __ led to an-oth-er. Now she's kiss-ing my mouth. __ I

Can you feel __ it? All the guys in here don't

e-ven wan-na dance. __ Can you feel _____ it? All that I can hear is